THE

PLEASURES OF THE COUNTRY:

Simple

STORIES FOR YOUNG PEOPLE,

BY

MRS. HARRIET MYRTLE.

———o———

WITH EIGHT ILLUSTRATIONS BY JOHN GILBERT.

London:
CUNDALL & ADDEY, 21, OLD BOND STREET.

———

1851.

A VISIT TO THE OLD HALL.

CONTENTS.

ILLUSTRATIONS.

———◆———

A VISIT TO THE OLD HALL.

EDWARD and KATE lived in a country town. It was a cheerful, clean town, with wide streets, and an old church that had large trees round it, and ivy growing up the tower. Their house had a garden behind it, in which they used to play very happily, drive their hoops round the walks, and run and jump about on the grass-plot. They also made many pleasant little excursions into the country round, when their sister Laura was able to go with them.

One of their favourite walks was through the woods belonging to an ancient manor-house, always called "The Old Hall," about a mile from the town. It belonged to a rich nobleman; but nobody had lived in it for a long time. The gardens and park were, however, kept in fine order; and it was said, that some day the house

B

would be put in repair and furnished. As it was now, people could walk by the paths through the woods close up to it.

One of these paths was just outside the wall of the flower garden, and led up to the portico of a sort of summer house or pavilion, partly gone to ruin. The door of this pavilion was always closed; but it was so shady and pleasant all round there, that it was a favourite place for Edward and Kate to play in, while Laura sat under a tree reading; and they would often look up at the beautiful roses, jasmines, and other creepers that hung over the top of the wall, and wish they might go into the garden and see all the lovely flowers they thought must be there.

They longed the more to be admitted within the wall, and see not only the garden, but the Old Hall itself, because a young carpenter, who was at work for their papa, putting up a book-case, had told them a great deal about it. This carpenter, John Wilson, was a great friend of theirs. He made a whole fleet of boats for them, which they sailed in the water-butt, in the garden, and taught them how to saw, and plane, and knock in nails; and while all this was going on, he would describe the painted windows and carved ceilings and walls in the Old Hall; and he knew all its wonders quite well, for he had worked there for several months, repairing some parts of the rooms that were going to destruction; and he said he hoped his lordship would soon have it all thoroughly done, and that he should be employed to do the work.

After all this, Kate and Edward were quite pleased, when, one day, John brought them permission to go and see it, from Mrs. Hollis, the housekeeper, who lived in one of the lodges, and was allowed to shew the place to visitors. If they went to the door of the pavilion in their favourite path, and rung the bell, she would admit them, he said. They thanked John very much for getting such a pleasure for them, and then ran to their mama to ask her leave to go, which she gave them directly; and, as the next day was very fine, they set out after their early dinner, in high spirits, accompanied by Laura. To add to their pleasure, their mama had told them they might order a donkey-chaise in the village, near the Hall gates, to bring them home, because she was sure they would be tired; and this was a thing they enjoyed extremely.

"Since you are going into the village, Master Edward, will you be so kind as to ask at the post-office if there's a letter for me?" said John Wilson, when Edward went to bid him good-bye. "Perhaps you will bring me good luck."

Edward readily promised to ask for the letter, and then whispered to Kate, "It's from his father he wants to hear, I know. He told me he should never be happy till he did. I wish we could bring him one."

But it was of no use to wish. There was no letter for John Wilson. So they ordered the donkey-chaise to be at the pavilion in three hours, and went on to the appointed place, and rang the bell.

Mrs. Hollis did not keep them long waiting; and when she came, she looked at them very kindly, and asked them to walk in. She was a formal little old lady, with a black silk gown on, that rustled as she moved, and wore a very white starched cap and handkerchief.

They liked the inside of the pavilion very much. The floor they trod on was made of squares of black and white marble, and there were seats and a round marble table. A long flight of white polished steps in front of it led down to a broad gravel walk that bounded one end of the flower garden. The garden was curiously laid out, in an old-fashioned style, and the green lawn in the middle looked so smooth and tempting, that they could not resist running down the steps towards it the moment they saw it; and Mrs. Hollis and Laura followed them.

Their feet sank in the thick velvet-like grass as they walked over it. In the middle there was a large round pond, with a fountain which sprung up into the air and then fell again in showers of sparkling drops, that ruffled the surface of the water, and made it glance in the sun as if it were all over diamonds. It was so clear, that, though it was deep, they could see every blade and leaf of the green mossy weeds among the white pebbles at the bottom; and presently they saw skimming through it a shoal of gold and silver fish. Little Kate had a slice of bread in the pocket of her apron, that her mama had given her in case they should feel hungry before they got home; so, as Mrs. Hollis told her the fish would come up to the surface to eat crumbs, she quickly threw some in for them, and up they came, one after another, and swallowed the pieces in their gaping mouths, while their bright scales flashed like fire as they caught the sunlight.

It was some time before the children could leave this delightful pond; but when they did, they saw that at each end there was a smaller one, both of which had their fountains, that sprung up, as if in imitation of the larger one; and that, between the centre pond and each of these, there was a large oval flower bed, and, at all the four corners of the lawn, a round one. These flower beds were bordered with ivy, so carefully pegged down that it formed thick wreaths of dark-green leaves, and made a beautiful setting for the bright flowers within. White lilies, tiger lilies, and tall lupins were in the middle; carnations, white and scarlet geraniums round them, with brilliant blue salvias, mignonette, fuchsias, and many other lovely things. Besides these beds, there were at regular distances tree roses on the lawn, with round bushy heads, full of splendid flowers of many different shades, sending out the most delicious scent; and the wall which bounded the gravel walk, and which they had so often looked at from the outside, was covered with all manner of creepers, trained roses, honeysuckle, maurandia, jasmine, passion-flowers, and many others.

As soon as they could make up their minds to go out of this bright garden, Mrs. Hollis shewed them that one side of it was formed by a wing of the house, and that large windows opened into it: but these were all shut at present; so she led them by a gateway in the wall to a long straight walk, which led under two tall cedar trees, whose branches met over their heads, to the principal entrance of the mansion. She then, with a large key which hung from her waist, together with several smaller ones, opened the great heavy door, and they all went in.

At first the light seemed so dim that they scarcely saw well around them; for their eyes had been looking at bright flowers, sparkling waters, and green trees and grass basking in the sun; but they soon saw that they were in a lofty square entrance hall, with beautiful painted glass windows, that threw rich colours, blue, red, purple, yellow, and green on the marble floor; and that the stone frames of the windows were carved and ornamented, and the stone walls and roof also; and that iron and steel armour of knights, with lances and helmets, were ranged in niches round the walls; and that long galleries, with many doors into different rooms, and more painted windows, went off on each side; and that, opposite to them was a wide staircase, all the steps of which were of dark oak, with carved rails, on the top of which were figures of animals reared up on their hind legs, and wreaths of fruit and flowers all carved in dark oak.

Then they went through many large rooms, with walls and ceilings of the same dark oak, beautifully carved in squares and other forms, to represent flowers and fruit, birds, and angels with wings; and these rooms had immense fire-places without grates, meant to burn logs of wood. Kate and Edward went under the richly ornamented mantel-pieces and looked up the wide chimneys. Then the windows—they liked them better than all; for the walls were so thick that each window seemed to be at the end of a little room of its own; and others were bay windows, and these seemed to be in still larger rooms; and the frames were richly carved; and they looked over the wide park with its green slopes and spreading trees, sweeping the grass with their long branches, and towering up towards the bright blue sky, and casting deep shadows on the sunny grass; and a clear river went winding among them; and all looked so lovely, that every time the children passed one of these windows, it seemed to them that they saw a new picture set in a dark frame.

At last, when they had gone through so many rooms,

that they began to keep very close to Laura, lest they should be lost, and had been up the wide staircase and through other rooms above, they heard, with joy, that they were next to go into the park. They followed Mrs. Hollis through a court and an old gateway, and here she bid them good-bye; and, after thanking her with all their hearts for her kindness, they turned round, and lost not a moment, but away they ran over the grass to the banks of the river.

It was delightful to stand in the shade and watch the running water rippling and tinkling over rocky stones that had the brightest green moss on them; and to see the taper points of the weeping willows, that dipped in the stream, and were always waving and trembling as it carried them with it. Sometimes a trout or perch would dart through the deep parts and disappear in an instant. They threw leaves and little sticks in, and watched them sailing away, and wished they had brought some of John's boats with them; then they dipped in their hands to feel the cool refreshing water glide through their fingers. Suddenly there appeared round a point two lovely white swans. On they came, arching their necks and ruffling their wings. Kate took out her bread again, and threw piece after piece to them, till all was gone, while they swam about catching them in their black beaks.

Now Laura called to the children to look at the trees. What great trees they were! Those round the church, which they had thought so large, would only make one arm of these. They crept under the branches of the beeches and limes, and there they were in a green little world,—green leaves above and all round, and green grass under foot, and the flickering sunlight peeping through upon them. Then they crept out again, and clambered up steep knolls, and ran down sloping banks, and every now and then stopped in wonder before some giant tree, with an enormous trunk, that, when they took hold of each other's hands, and then Laura's, and all three stretched out their arms to the utmost, they had still not grasped half of. They could not decide which kind of tree was the most beautiful,—the oak, with its rough bark, strong arms, and deep rich green; the beech, with smooth, shining stem and graceful, sweeping branches; the tufted elms; or the limes, so light and feathery. Then there were Spanish chesnuts, and horse-chesnuts, and dark firs, and birches with bark as white as silver. It was impossible to know which was most beautiful.

Now they wound round a woody hill, into a beautiful glade, and came upon the whole herd of deer, pretty spotted creatures, some with branching horns, some grazing, some lying in the shade. Quietly as the children tried to get near them, they were startled, and bounded off like lightning, but did not go very far, and continued in sight for some time.

The walk through the park had taken a good while, and the children began to feel tired; so Laura persuaded them to sit down and rest on a pleasant bank, all overgrown with wreaths of periwinkle, with its pretty blue flowers. While they sat, there came past, like a stately lady in a court dress, a splendid peacock, his gorgeous tail sweeping the ground, his crested head erect, and his lovely neck glancing purple, green, and gold. Then came another, and another, and then several pea-hens, not so showy, but very graceful in form. Kate wished she had kept some bread for them; but they seemed to be satisfied with admiration; and one of them spread his tail up like a fan, as if to please them, and displayed all its brilliant eyes, that shone like gold and gems in the sun.

c 2

When the peacocks had passed on, Kate began to wish she had kept a little bread for herself and Edward, for the walk had been long, and she felt hungry. Edward declared he was more thirsty than hungry, but consoled himself with the thoughts of the nice drive home in the donkey-chaise. They had made the circuit of the park, and were close to the garden wall, and the gardener's house, which stood at one corner of it; so Laura, who was always kind, went to the door and asked if she could buy a little milk. The gardener's wife said she would sell her some, and also let her buy a few home-baked cakes, and lent her a bowl, and spoon, and plate, and said, if the young lady and gentleman would like to sit down in the pavilion above the garden and take their refreshment there, they might leave all these things on the marble table, and she could easily fetch them away by and bye. This was a very pleasant idea, and away they went merrily up the gravel walk to enjoy their feast. They took off their straw hats when they reached the shady pavilion, that they might feel the cool air, and poured out their milk; but before tasting it, they went to the door to see if the donkey-chaise had come.

It was not there yet; but, looking round, they saw lying

by the path an old man, who seemed to be asleep, and who rested his head on the lap of a young girl sitting by his side. She was leaning her head on her hand, and had not heard the children come to the door; for she seemed filled with sad thoughts, and tears kept dropping through her fingers.

Kate and Edward stood with pitying looks on the steps, when the old man raised his head, but seemed too weary to open his eyes, and said in a feeble voice,

"We must go on, Martha."

"Are you any better, father?" said she, wiping her tears away.

"Not much—hunger and sorrow are bad nurses, dear," he replied; "but night will come upon us before we get to any place to sleep in, if we do not move on."

"Poor old man! He is tired and hungry, and has got nothing to eat," whispered little Kate to Edward; and the tears came into her eyes. "*I* am not at all hungry now: are you?"

"Let us go and bring the milk to them," Edward answered.

They ran to their table; and while Kate took up the bowl of milk, and, carefully holding it in both hands, carried it to the door, Edward brought the plate of cakes, and Laura followed, wondering what they were going to do.

The young girl had already risen from her seat; the old man was sitting up, and looked sadly pale and tired.

"Will you drink this milk?" said Kate, raising her eyes to his face, while Edward held the plate of cakes to him.

"God bless you, little angels," said the old man. "He has sent you to help us in our sore need."

"Oh! thank and bless you, kind young lady and gentleman," cried his daughter.

"Drink some first, Martha, my child," said her father, taking the bowl and holding it towards her. She obeyed him, and seemed to enjoy the draught, as if she had wanted it very much indeed; and then he drank, and it seemed to do him so much good that the children felt quite joyous as they looked at them both.

"Now eat the cakes," said Edward; and as soon as each had taken one he set the plate down, that they might not be hurried, and ran to get the hats, for the donkey-chaise drove up at the moment.

Laura kissed her little brother and sister very affectionately, as she tied their hats for them, and then asked the old man if he and his daughter had far to go?

He said they were still thirty miles from home, and that they had walked all the way from London, where they had gone hoping to get some money that was owing him, and besides, to meet his son, whose ship was expected; but he had been disappointed in both his hopes, and, what was worse, he feared his poor boy's ship had been wrecked, and he should never see him again.

"Poor sailor boy!" said Kate.

"But do not despair," said Laura. "If you had waited a little longer he might have come."

"I waited too long," he replied; "for our money is all spent,—we have none left, and only trust to selling a few balls and pin-cushions my poor girl has made, to get a lodging to-night, and a bit of bread to-morrow."

"And have you no other son?" asked Laura.

"I have another, Lady, said he;" but he's the same as dead to me. He got into wild ways after he had served his apprenticeship, and I was harsh to him, and he left his home, and I have never heard of him since. Many misfortunes fell on me afterwards. Yes, yes, I was too harsh."

The old man looked down gloomily. In a minute, however, he raised his head and said, "But God bless you for your kind hearts; we are so refreshed by this sweet milk and these cakes, that we shall walk on to Summerton quite heartily. It's the nearest town, they tell me."

As he spoke he got up, and bowing respectfully to Laura, and smiling gratefully to the children, who were busy putting all the things belonging to the gardener's wife where she had directed, he began to walk away; but he walked quite feebly, and poor Martha's shoes were worn out, and she limped as she followed him.

Little Kate had just taken her seat in the donkey-chaise.

"How tired they look!" said she, as she saw them going slowly on.

"I will run after them, and direct them to our house," said Laura. "I am sure mama will help them to a night's lodging."

"And Laura, dear," said Kate, getting out of the chaise, "if Edward does not mind walking, I don't; so tell them—shall we Edward?—to get in instead of us."

"Yes, yes," said Edward, eagerly.

"That I will, dear children," Laura answered; and,

stopping the old man and his daughter, she succeeded, after a great deal of persuasion, in making them accept the children's offer, and then helped them in.

Much as they liked a drive in a donkey-chaise, no drive in the world could have made these children so happy as they felt in their walk home. Their hearts full of joy, they bounded along, jumping over tree stumps, running up and down banks, and never thinking of either fatigue, hunger, or thirst.

"Here we come, John," they cried, as they approached their own door, and saw John coming out after his day's work, his basket on his shoulder.

The donkey-chaise had got behind in climbing the hill at the entrance of the town, but it came up at this moment. John's basket fell from his hand, and fell heavily on the door-step, and he rushed towards it, crying,

"Father! father! how is it I see you here?"

"John,—my dear son!" cried the old man; and they grasped each other by both hands, and seemed to search in each other's faces for answers to many questions; and then Martha took hold of her brother's arm, and he remembered her, changed as she was from the merry, rosy girl he had left her.

"Come home with me, father, and my poor Martha," said John; "and please God you shall never know want more. If I had known you were come to poverty, never would I have waited for a letter of pardon before I went home to you."

"It is all along of those dear, blessed children, that fed us when we were hungry and thirsty, and sent us on in their chaise when we were weary, that we have found you now."

John gave his little friends a look of gratitude that said more than many words; and then, all bidding good-night, they separated, the old man and Martha going home with him, and the children running to their mama to tell her all the adventures of this happy day, round their cheerful tea-table. They now understood why John was so anxious for a letter, and why he never received it, because his father had gone to London.

Next evening they went to see him, and found him at supper with his father and sister, who were dressed in nice new clothes, and looked much better and happier. They all welcomed Kate and Edward joyfully, and gave them seats, and John went into his little garden, in which he worked at his spare hours, and picked them a dish of fine ripe strawberries, which they enjoyed very much.

A week afterwards, John went to his father's village to sell off his furniture, and give up his cottage, for they had resolved to live all together in Summerton. Kate and Edward went to his house the evening he was expected home, and stood at the door watching for him, while Martha got tea ready, and her father swept up the hearth.

"Here he comes!" cried Edward, who saw him first.

"And there's a sailor-boy with him," cried Kate.

Now there was a joyful meeting. John had found his brother on the road to his father's village. His ship had come into port two days before.

The old man used to say afterwards, when he looked back to this time, that everything went well with him from the moment he saw the faces of those dear children; and they always remembered the day when they visited the Old Hall, as one of the happiest of their lives.

As for the fine Old Hall, John's hope was fulfilled about it. His lordship had it repaired and furnished, and came to live there, and made John his head carpenter there; so that he never wanted work, and in time took his brother into partnership, and the two sons made their father and sister happy and comfortable all their days.

THE PICNIC IN THE FOREST.

A PIC-NIC IN THE FOREST.

"It must be six o' clock!" cried Florence Thornhill, starting up in bed; "and it is a lovely morning. Emily, it *must* be six o'clock."

"Has Jane called us?" said Emily, almost in her sleep.

"No: but—hush! One, two, three, four. Oh! the clock only struck four;" and Florence fell fast asleep in an instant.

In another hour she jumped up again. "It must be"— the clock began to strike as she spoke, and she counted, "one, two, three, four, five,—only five yet," and once more fell asleep.

All was quiet till, another hour having past, Jane came in saying, "It is just going to strike six, young ladies."

Florence was up in an instant, and Emily soon after her. They had been invited by their friends, Mr. and

Mrs. Grove, who lived on the borders of Epping Forest, to join a young party who were to spend the whole day in the Forest, and to carry provisions with them and dine there. To Florence and Emily, who lived in London, this was a delightful prospect. They had thought of nothing else for a week. They were quickly dressed, ran down to breakfast, and before it was over, the carriage that was to take them to the railway was at the door. Their papa and mama wished them a very happy day, and they soon drove off, accompanied by Jane, to take care of them; a basket containing a large cake and a cold pie, their mama's contribution to the feast, being put in and given to Jane's charge.

Fast as they drove, it was not fast enough to satisfy their impatience. Florence especially was "quite certain" they should be too late, and stretched out her head to look at every clock they passed. They were, however, in excellent time, and in a few minutes they were seated in the train. Off they set; and even to them it seemed wonderfully soon when they stopped at the station, and heard a voice at the window ask, "Are the Miss Thorn-hills here?"

It was Mrs. Grove's coachman; and there was Ernest,

her youngest little boy, waiting in the open carriage. They were soon seated by his side, Jane by the coachman, and away they drove again.

It was a lovely morning in August. The sky was bright blue, with a few heavy white clouds sailing over it; but Jacob the coachman, who was anxiously questioned, and who looked very grave and wise, declared there would be no rain. The air felt deliciously fresh to the two little London girls. They thought the cottages looked very clean and pretty; then the gardens were gay with dahlias and hollyhocks, the orchards full of red-cheeked apples, and a pleasant smell of wood smoke every now and then in the air. They had twenty questions to ask of Ernest, and at every house they came to, they said, "Is this your house now?"

At last they stopped at a white gate. It was thrown open directly by Fred, Ernest's elder brother, who had been watching for them; and at the sound of the wheels, his two sisters, Annie and Jessy, came running out to receive them, followed by two little boys, whose names were Alfred and Johnny, who had come to join the party; and behind all came bounding and barking, Dash the dog.

When they stopped at the door they thought this was

the prettiest house of any they had seen yet. The porch was covered with clematis and jasmine, and the borders and beds full of bright flowers. Out of the porch came Mr. and Mrs. Grove, and kissed and welcomed them, and told them that they were all ready to start for the Forest.

So much the better. They longed to be there. The contents of the basket were quickly transferred to a certain large pannier that stood in the lobby; Jane was recommended to the care of the maids, who promised to take her a nice walk; and in a little while the whole happy party was on the road to the Forest, Mr. Grove leading the way, because it was declared that he knew the prettiest paths. He took them up a wooded bank among straggling trees.

"Emily and Florence must shut their eyes now," cried Annie; "I will lead them."

"No, you take Emily and I will lead Florence," said Ernest.

Both shut their eyes and followed to the top of the bank.

"Now you may look."

They opened their eyes. Below them lay the fine old Forest. It looked like a whole ocean of green tree tops, stretching miles and miles to right and left, filling all the valley before them, and clothing the ridge of the opposite hill till they were lost against the sky. A narrow winding path at their feet dived down into this green world, and down it in a moment ran all with joyous shouts. In half a minute they could see nothing on every side of them but trees.

The trees were of the strangest shapes: very short, with bushy heads, and stems that leaned all manner of ways and were knotted and mossy, and sometimes they looked like curious wood creatures dancing. They were so close together that their branches met over head, and formed a thick roof of leaves. Long wreaths of ivy and honeysuckle twined about them, and great ferns grew among them, often taller than the trees themselves; because they were allowed to grow as they liked, but the trees were lopped every few years to supply wood to all the people that lived near. Round about these twisted stems, and among these tangled under-growths, the children ran and danced, sometimes stopping to gather a pretty bluebell, or some bright berries, or to peep into a deserted bird's nest, or look at some insect, Mr. Grove only warning them to keep near the path lest they should be lost.

E

"O come into this lovely arbour," cried Emily, stopping before a group of trees, where the branches had met over head, and then drooped downwards, leaving a hollow in the middle. As she stooped to look in, a rabbit, which had been asleep there, rushed out, and scudded away, with Dash after it, barking and yelping. But Dash soon came back, hanging out his tongue, and looking rather foolish, for the rabbit had found his hole near, and was safe in it in a minute.

The children all crept into Emily's arbour, and nestled within it very comfortably.

"Now tell us a story, Annie," said little Ernest.

"O yes," said Florence; "something about a fairy that lived in the trees, or—"

Just then something rustled the branches over head, and a black cow, with a white face and large horns, looked down upon them.

"Oh! Oh!" exclaimed Florence, and began to make her way out at the opposite side of the thicket.

"It's only a cow. It will not hurt you," cried Fred and Annie at once. But she was not used to be so near a cow, and made her way out, coming bounce against a large pig that was lying under a hazel tree on its side.

"Ouf! Ouf!" grunted the pig, and, scrambling up, he began to move off, but presently turned round, and looked at her as if it had occurred to him, on reflection, that she had no right to disturb him.

"Come and drive away this great pig, Freddy," she cried.

That was soon done. Away galloped the pig, crushing the thick branches under his hoofs.

They had all crept out after Florence, and the path on that side looked so pretty that Annie called to her papa to ask him to lead them down it. It went winding among beech trees, which, when they were lopped, had thrown out long feathery branches from their roots and stems, making a beautiful green wall on each side, and meeting in an arch above. As they walked along it, they saw many and many another, quite as beautiful, branching off in all directions, like endless shrubberies, and were often tempted to run down them, but for the fear of losing themselves.

"What is that tinkling bell I hear every now and then?" asked Emily.

"That is a bell round a cow's neck," answered Mrs. Grove. "The cow that startled Florence so much had probably twenty companions feeding near us, and one or two always have bells to guide their owners where to find them at milking time."

"And were there a number of pigs too?" asked Florence.

"There are great numbers in the Forest. Nearly all the cottagers keep them, and let them roam about in search of roots and nuts; but they are unsocial creatures, and seldom feed together. In the evenings you may see them, one by one, issuing from the several paths out of the trees, and each making his way to his own home. There they stand grunting and squeaking at the door of their styes till some one lets them in.

"How funny they must look!" said Florence, laughing.

"But how sensible of them!" said Emily. "I had no idea pigs were so clever. I am sure I should not know the way out of the Forest."

The path had now led them to the borders of a clear little stream, flowing in the bottom of the valley, among stones and stumps covered with bright green moss. They crossed it and came to an open grassy space, where twenty or thirty rough, shaggy-looking horses were feeding; these only lifted their heads for a minute, to look at the visitors, and then went on eating.

Now they went along a green path, among bushes where the bright sun beamed down upon them.

"O look! what quantities of blackberries!" cried Alfred.

All were scattered among the brambles in a moment, enjoying the delights of blackberry gathering. The fruit hung ripe and black in large bunches; fingers and lips were soon dyed with the juice, and not a few stains and holes were made in frocks. Then Annie's basket was filled, that they might take some home for Jane.

Mr. Grove now called them all together; for it was time to go on. All were soon collected, except Jessie and Emily. They were called, but no answer came, and no one could see them anywhere.

"I will climb a tree and look out," said Fred. "I shall be sure to see them." Accordingly he climbed the highest he could find, and looked all round.

"I see them," he cried. "There they go, running exactly the wrong way. Holloa! Jessie! Emily! Stop!" And he took out his handkerchief and waved it.

All the children stood looking up anxiously. "Do they see you?" asked Mr. Grove.

"They have stopped and are looking about. They see

me now. Here they come," said Fred, beginning to slide down; and as he reached the ground they came running up quite out of breath, and rather frightened at the idea that they might have lost themselves.

They continued to walk for nearly half an hour near the stream, among scattered trees, stopping every now and then to gather long wreaths of briony, or honey-suckle, or ivy, or to watch the rabbits that started out of the bushes, or listen to a woodpigeon, or stock-dove at a distance, the only sounds that reached them in this silent place. At last they came to a grove of fine large trees, stretching as far as they could see in all directions. It looked almost dark in there, so great was the contrast with the sunny place in which they stood. The little stream took its course under the trees, which hung arch-ing over it; and by the path at its side they went in under the tall trees. As they entered they ceased to laugh and talk, and felt inclined to whisper. It was a beautiful place. The ground was brown with the leaves of last autumn; the branches met over head at a great height, and everywhere a green light was spread.

Presently they found a nook where the stream had been checked in its course by a fallen tree, and had collected into a round pool. On the bridge made by this tree all the children had soon seated themselves, watching the water foaming over one part where it had made a channel for itself, and glancing in the straggling sunbeams that came flickering through the leaves.

"Look at that squirrel peeping at us out of its nest," whispered Johnny.

Looking up, they saw, after a time, the round bright eye of a squirrel, high up in the tree over their heads, and soon they spied another at a little distance, fussing about among the leaves on the ground, finding nuts for his little ones. Perhaps they made some noise, for he took fright and climbed up a tall stem as quick as lightning, and then leaped to a tree opposite, through the air, where they could see him quite well, with his bushy brown tail curled above his head.

"Hush!" said Mr. Grove, at this moment. "Look there!"

They turned where he pointed, and saw come silently tripping along, one behind another, six or seven of the Forest deer. The children remained so still that the timid creatures never saw or heard them, but passed on among the trees out of sight.

A rustling among the leaves was now heard, as if some one was coming. Who should it be but Jacob the coach-man, leading the horse that had brought the carriage from the station, but who now bore two large panniers on his back, instead of drawing a carriage. The horse's name was Sir Toby.

"Here comes Jacob with Sir Toby. Is this where we are to dine, papa? O what a lovely place to dine in!" exclaimed several voices.

All collected round the panniers directly, and now mama took the direction of affairs.

"Fix on the spot where we shall lay the cloth," said she.

They scattered about to choose a place. One fixed here, another there; at last all agreed that the most beautiful had been found. It was a round space covered with soft grass, where the trees and bushes left just a sufficient opening. The stream running behind the bushes, but close by, would supply them with delicious water. Here, therefore, they fixed it should be.

The white tablecloth was spread smoothly, and looked very pretty with its green border of grass.

"Now Dash, take care of my shawl," said Annie.

"And of my bonnet," said Emily. Dash accordingly took his place beside the bonnet and shawl.

Jacob unpacked the mugs, and a tumbler, some spoons, knives, and forks, the salt and pepper. Annie, assisted by Alfred and Johnny, took all these things, put them down, and stationed herself at one end to direct the proceedings. A pile of plates came next. Emily placed these opposite to Annie; then a large jar of milk, which Jessie put by them.

"Who will carry this pie?" said Mrs. Grove.

"I will,—let *me*," said little Ernest; so it was trusted to him, and he brought it quite safely.

A round basket, piled with fruit, came next. There were grapes, peaches, apples, pears, and plums. Florence begged to carry the fruit, and it was put on her head, and she followed Ernest. Behind her came Fred with the cake.

While these were laid on the tablecloth, other things were coming out of the panniers,—cold fowls and ham, tarts and bread. When all was put down, it looked a splendid feast. They took their places. A tree stump was found for papa and mama, but the children chose to sit on the grass. Never was there a merrier party. Even Jacob, grave as he was, could not help smiling at

F

the shouts of laughter that reached him as he sat on a large stone, eating his plateful of cold pie, and letting Sir Toby feast on the short grass. The children carved, handed the plates, and managed everything. Mr. and Mrs. Grove were not allowed to take any trouble, but were waited on by all. There was a great deal to do, running to the stream for water, handing things round, changing the plates, and then clearing away, and giving the empty dishes to Jacob's charge to be packed. Dash was not forgotten, and seemed to enjoy himself very much. Afterwards they sat still for some time, and told stories, asked riddles, and sung songs.

"Now, Annie," said Mrs. Grove, rising as the last song ended, "your papa and I must go home, but we will leave you here to play for an hour or two. Jacob can remain, and will see you safely home."

They were delighted with this permission, and lost no time in beginning some games. They had "Follow my leader," "Hunt the hare," and then "Hide and seek." It was a capital place for this; there were hollow trees, thick bushes, and deep holes, and one after another hid and was found after a great deal of fun. At last it was Florence's turn. She seemed to have fixed on a very good place, for no one could find her. In vain they searched in every hole and stump, looked up trees where it was impossible she could have climbed, and into great bramble bushes, where she could not have crept without being scratched to pieces. Nearly two hours had passed since they began their games, and Jacob declared it was time to go home.

"Florence!" cried Emily, "where are you? come out: we ought to go home."

No answer.

"Florence! we give it up; we cannot find you;. where are you, Florence?" was shouted by every one.

Still no answer.

"It's not play, Flory; we are frightened," cried Emily. "Do speak."

All was still silent.

"Come and help us to look, Jacob," said Annie; and Jacob came, with his grave face, and began to beat the bushes, and peer about everywhere.

"Suppose we should never find her again!" said poor Emily, almost crying. "Dear Flory, do speak!" And she sat down on the grass with a feeling of fear, of she did not know what.

"It *must* be six o'clock, and it's a lovely morning," exclaimed a voice at her feet, and up started Florence from under a heap of dry leaves, where she had hidden, and felt so comfortable that she had fallen fast asleep.

"Here she is! Florence is found!" cried; Emily, in joy; and from all quarters the seekers came running to the spot, while Florence, hardly knowing where she was, stared round her in surprise.

Fred came up first: "Where had—?" he cried; but no more was heard, for he sunk into the ground and disappeared.

Johnny came next, running towards them: "So you are—" he began, and also sunk into the ground, and disappeared.

Alfred was next. "Ah, Florence! I am—" he sunk, and disappeared.

Florence started up, but when she had got on her knees she began slipping and sinking, and in an instant had vanished.

"What is it?—where are—?" cried Emily rushing forward, and sunk like the others.

"Bless me!" cried Jacob. "Stop a moment! Wait a bit, Miss Jessie; hold fast by that stump, Miss Annie!"

But both were running too fast to stop themselves, and when they set their feet on the spot where all the rest had vanished, down they went and disappeared.

Little Ernest had taken longer to come up than the rest, for he had been dreadfully frightened about Florence, and had gone to a great distance to seek her, and had seen all this with the greatest wonder. He was running fast towards the place, when Florence's head appeared above ground.

"Dear Florence!" he cried, holding out both his hands, and catching hold of her's, which now came above ground also, "where are you? Have you all tumbled into one of those ponds covered with leaves, papa told us about? Shall you all be drowned?"

He pulled her with all his might as he spoke, and she came safely up on firm ground beside him, laughing heartily.

"Drowned!" cried Fred, whose face now appeared; "I was never so comfortable in my life. It's like the softest bed, only a great deal nicer."

"I do not wonder Florence went to sleep;" said Alfred, whose head next came in sight. "We are in a pit full of nice dry leaves."

Jacob had, by this time, cut a long stick, which he held out to them, and by its help he got them out, after a great deal of laughing, with their hair stuck over with brown leaves.

"Yes, Jacob, we really will make haste and go home," said Annie, in answer to his representation that they should be very late. "But where's Dash?"

"Dash! Dash!" cried Fred.

Dash barked angrily in answer, from a distance, but did not come.

"Where's my bonnet?" said Emily.

"And my shawl?" said Annie. Dash barked angrily again. "O, now I remember. Poor Dash! He is watching them all this time!" They ran back to the place where they had dined, and there they found him at his post, the bonnet and shawl on one side, and the basket of blackberries on the other. He was praised and patted till he had quite forgotten his anger, and was up and ready for anything again.

"Now then, where are the panniers and Sir Toby?" said Annie.

"Here are the panniers all ready packed, Miss Annie," answered Jacob; "but, bless me! where's Sir Toby?"

They looked all round, and presently discovered Sir Toby trotting very contentedly along the path homewards. He had gone nearly out of sight already.

"Bless me!" exclaimed poor Jacob again, "what shall I do? I cannot leave you young ladies and gentlemen alone. Wo there! Wo there! The horse will not stop. He may come to mischief."

"Run after him, Jacob," cried Fred. "We will stay by the panniers."

Jacob ran on. They thought he would succeed at first, for Sir Toby stopped to eat, but no sooner did he hear Jacob behind him, than he pricked up his ears and trotted on again. It was impossible to help laughing, troublesome as it was. How to get home all the heavy things they could not think. Fred ran on a little way to see if he could do anything to help. Turning the corner of a thicket, he came against a donkey feeding, and saw behind the trees a little cottage, with a great stack of wood by it much higher than itself. An old woman stood at the door.

"Is that your horse yonder, running away, Master?" said she; and she looked so good-natured, that he told her all the case.

"If our donkey will do to carry the panniers he shall go with you," said she, "and my son can lead him and bring him back."

Fred thanked her heartily, and then made signs to Jacob to go on again. Jacob had begun to run back, despairing of stopping Sir Toby, and distracted between his duty to the young ladies and gentlemen and the horse.

"Go after your horse!" shouted the old woman, pointing energetically along the path. Seeing he still doubted, she led the donkey up a steep bank and pushed her son to his head. Jacob understood; he saw that this stout country lad and this donkey would supply the place of himself and Sir Toby, and with a heart eased of half its load of care, he started off again in pursuit.

The donkey was soon loaded, not forgetting the blackberries, and the whole party moved homewards after many thanks to the kind old woman, who promised to come up to tea and return with her son. Sir Toby was safe in his stable when they arrived. He had gone straight to the door and waited there for Jacob.

Tea was ready in the pretty drawing-room; and when they were going to take their places round the table, with clean hands and faces, hair brushed smooth, and holes mended up as well as they could be in a hurry, the door opened and in came Mr. and Mrs. Thornhill. Here was joy for Emily and Florence. It was to meet them Mr. Grove had left the Forest; and when it was announced that, instead of going away next morning, they were all to remain together for a week, the pleasure was complete. The adventures of the day were talked over, and seemed to give as much enjoyment, now they were remembered, as when they were actually happening; and, better than all, they could look forward to many more such happy days, for they had a whole week before them. Emily and Florence felt how delightful it would be to take their papa and mama to the beautiful places, and shew them where they saw the cows, and pigs, and the other creatures, and where they picked blackberries, and where they dined, and, above all, the pit of dry leaves; and Mr. Grove declared that he could lead them to many other places, and through many more paths, quite as beautiful as those they had already seen in the old Forest.

GRANDPAPA'S HAY-FIELD.

WHEN the trees were green, and the hedges full of wild roses, and birds singing, and butterflies fluttering over the sweet clover-fields, in the pleasant month of June, Willie and Alice Grey received an invitation to go to their grandpapa's on the last day of hay-making, when the hay is carted and stacked. Their grandpapa had a garden, a field, and a cow, and a swing in the field; and at all times, to go to see him and their aunts was a great pleasure, but at hay-making time it was more than ever delightful; so they set out with their mama and their favourite dog Ranger, in joyous spirits.

It was a bright sunny morning and very warm, and the road was very dusty, so that, happy as they were, they could not help feeling tired before half the walk was over; and when they came in sight of Farmer Dale's, they

GRANDPAPA'S HAY-FIELD

wished "this was grandpapa's," and sat down by the gate,
thinking it would be very nice if they might go by the
fields instead of the dusty road. At this moment they
heard the sound of wheels, and horses' feet coming tramp,
tramp behind the hedge, and, looking through the gate,
they saw Farmer Dale's horse and wagon with Charley
the carter walking by the side.

"Ah Charley!" cried little Willie, "where are you
going?"

"To Squire Wakefield's," answered he, "to cart his hay."

"Then we shall see you again presently, for we are
going to grandpapa's too," said Willie.

"Wo! Smiler," said Charley, and the horse stopped.

Charley began to open the gate, then touched his hat,
and asked Mrs. Grey if she would please to walk in and go
through the fields. She was very much obliged to him,
and the children were delighted to get on the grass.
They ran along by the side of the cart, looking at the
great horse as he went on so strongly, and as if he did
not feel the weight of the cart in the least.

"What is all that wood for, that you have in the
wagon?" asked Alice.

"That is to lay under the hay-stack. The hay is laid

on wood, not on the damp ground, you see, Miss. If it was not for the wood, you and Master Willie might have got into the cart and had a ride, but you might get hurt some way if it shook about."

"Thank you, Charley; I should have liked it very much," said she.

"Wo! Smiler," said Charley again, and again Smiler stopped.

"You could both ride on Smiler's back, if you're not afraid," said Charley.

"May we, mama?" cried Alice. "I should like it very much, only it looks so high up."

"Suppose we should tumble off," said little Willie, rather doubtfully.

Their mama was a little afraid at first too, but Charley assured her he would take great care of the young gentleman and lady; and presently Willie felt quite courageous, and was lifted up and seated very firmly, and took fast hold of the collar. Then Charley lifted up Alice, and she put her arm round Willie's waist. Then Ranger began to bark and leap up as if he wanted to have a ride too.

"Stay by us, mama," cried Willie. "What a height we are from the ground!"

"Oh yes, stay by us," said Alice, who could not help feeling a little frightened too.

"I will stay by you," said their mama; "sit firm, and you are in no danger."

"Now hold fast," cried Charley. "Gee wot! Smiler!" and away went Smiler, tramp, tramp again. Very soon they got used to the motion, and laughed and chatted, and enjoyed it very much. Ranger went on, jumping and barking all the way; but Smiler did not mind: he never stopped. It was all their mama could do to keep up with them.

"Open the gate. Look where we are," cried Willie, when they stopped at their grandpapa's field, and smelt the sweet new hay. The gate was thrown open, and in they went in triumph, and were soon surrounded by a whole troop of merry people, with hay-forks and rakes in their hands, and lifted down and kissed and welcomed by all.

There were Aunt Lucy, and Aunt Emily, and Uncle John, and there were their little cousins Mary and Janey, with their elder brother Robert, and their friends Herbert and Meggy, with their papa and mama. And there were Thomas, the gardener, and two hay-makers, whose names were Joe and Roger, and Emma, the cook, and Harriet, the housemaid.   All were in the field, hard at work, spreading the large hay-cocks into long ridges ready to cart.

Willie and Alice were first taken to the summer-house, in one corner of the field, to have some cake and milk, and then a little rake was given to each, and they went hard to work raking the hay like the rest.

The wagon was standing behind the summer-house, by the place where the stack was to be made, and Thomas was busy unloading it, and laying the wood in a proper form, ready to lay the hay on. This was soon done, and he got into the wagon himself, fork in hand.

"Who will have a ride down the field?" he cried.

"I will,—I will,—let me,—take me up," cried many voices, and in two minutes every child there was seated in the wagon, and away went Smiler with them down the field, and Charley led him to the end of one of the long ridges of hay.

Now out they must all come as fast as they got in. Uncle John held out his hands, and jumped them down one after another, on to the ridge of hay, and ended by burying them under it. But Thomas called out, that it was not time to play yet, so they all scrambled up as well as they could for laughing. Joe and Roger, Uncle John and Robert, forked up the hay and threw it into the wagon, and Thomas, standing up in it, packed it all even; all the rest raked after them, collecting what was scattered, and Charley led Smiler on and on, as they cleared. Soon there was a good heaped load.

"Who will have a ride on the top of the hay?" cries Thomas.

All the children were ready. So now Uncle John must lift them up, and, as Thomas received them, and seated them on the dry loose hay, they sunk in it very comfortably, and their faces peeped out like the young birds in a nest. When Smiler moved on they set up a shout, and grandpapa himself came out to see what was doing.

"Here we are! Ah, grandpapa, come up too!" cried Alice and Willie; but he laughed, and said, "that would never do for him."

Now they had to be handed down again, sliding and jumping as well as they could; for the wagon was led to the right place, and the hay was to be forked out and laid in order on the wood. Joe and Roger built the stack; Thomas, Robert, and Uncle John threw the hay out of the wagon; the rest had time to rest or play; only a few had to rake what was scattered by the wind or dropped, and Thomas soon sent them all to shake the rest of the cocks into ridges.

Now came a new visitor into the field: it was Daisy, the cow. All the time the grass was growing, she had been kept in the cow-house, but now Aunt Lucy had determined she should come and enjoy the pleasant air and grass once more. Daisy was a pretty Guernsey cow, with short horns, a small head, short legs, and was prettily spotted white and light brown. She was very gentle and tame, but she was young and playful; so when she found herself once more in her field, she set off, levelled her horns at a large hay-cock, knocked it down, and ran round by the hedge with a great bunch of hay on her head. Everybody laughed, and grandpapa declared it was exactly as if she had said to the hay-cock, "So it was for you I was kept shut up all this time! down with you!"

"You ought to have jumped over it, Daisy!" cried Uncle John.

"Uncle John must jump over a hay-cock!" cried Alice.

"Yes, yes, Uncle John. *Do* jump over a hay-cock," exclaimed several voices.

"To be sure I will," he said; so he laid down his fork, took off his straw hat, chose out one of the tallest hay-cocks, went back several paces, took a run, then a jump; but, high as he jumped, it was not high enough. His foot came thump against the top of the hay-cock, knocked it off, and he tumbled down on the other side, where he was buried under the rest of it by the children the next minute.

There is no saying when he would have got out; but the sight of the empty wagon, going down the field, made them all eager for a ride, and Uncle John must crawl out and help them in; and then every one was hard at work again.

By-and-by it was dinner time. A cold dinner was ready for every one, and it was surprising what appetites they had; but the children could not sit long,—they must be off to the field again; and as the men were not ready to go on yet, they began to play. They pelted each other with hay. Little Willie was seized as he was running along with a load on his head to throw at some one, laid on a hay-cock, and quite hid under a heap; then out he got, and Alice was smothered, then all the others.

H

"Would anybody like a swing?" cried Robert, who had just come out.

Everybody liked swinging, so to the swing all went. It was hung to one of the arms of a large elm tree. Alice was put in first, and Robert swung her so high that she touched the green leaves and branches with her feet, and she enjoyed it very much; but she soon called out to him to stop, that some one else might come in. Herbert was such a bold swinger that he liked to stand up on the board, and Janey stood up with him; they held tight, and went up as high as Alice had done. Then little Willie and Mary were put in side by side, and swung together, and then Meggy had her turn; and while she was scudding through the air, first touching the high branches with her head, then with the tips of her toes, Thomas called all to work again.

Smiler had been taken out of the shafts and allowed to feed where he liked, but now he must be fastened in again; and as Charley had gone a message, Joe undertook to do it, and was a long time over it, for he did not understand how to fasten the buckles; however, it was done at last, and he led the wagon while the others loaded, and then the children were mounted on the top as before. They had got to the lower part of the field, and Smiler had to drag them up a steep bank. As he was straining up, and had nearly reached the top, one of the buckles, not properly fastened by Joe, gave way. Up went the shafts, down went the back of the wagon, and out fell all the hay and all the children with it on the grass. Smiler walked off quietly, and began to eat grass very contentedly; grandpapa, uncle, aunts, papas, and mamas rushed to the spot in alarm. Nothing was to be seen of children, nothing but a great heap of hay; but the hay began to shake, and out came a head, then a foot, then a hand, then several heads, feet, and hands; then some were able to laugh, others to cry, and others to answer the anxious question, " Are you hurt?"

No one was hurt. Alice's bonnet was beat flat over her eyes, but her mama soon straightened it; Meggy's frock was torn, but Aunt Emily brought out a needle and thread and mended it; Herbert lost a top out of his pocket, and Willie could not find his cap till the hay was nearly all flung into the wagon again; but when they had shaken themselves well, and had got the hay out of their mouths and hair as well as they could, it was declared that no harm was done. It happened, however, that though Charley now fastened the harness right and tight, no one asked to get up on the next load or two; they preferred rather to run by the side.

The sun began to go round towards the west, and the trees to cast a longer shadow, and the field was nearly cleared; but now tea was ready under a spreading beech. Such a great tea-pot, such an immense jug of milk, such platefuls of cake and bread and butter, such piled heaps of strawberries and cherries were there for them, as they had never seen before; and much they enjoyed everything.

"What are those bright ribbons for, Aunt Lucy?" cried somebody. And, all leaving the remains of the feast, found the grass covered with bits of ribbon of every colour.

"Where are your rakes?" said she. "Choose your colours. All of you must have a streamer on your rakes when the last load goes to be stacked."

Now there was a great bustle. One would have green, another blue, another pink, another white. Then the forks were dressed; and then, for papas and mamas, who had not been at work, long sticks were cut, and ribbons tied on them. Smiler must be dressed now. He had bunches of green leaves at each ear; and, as ribbon failed, long strips of bright-coloured calico were torn up and tied about his mane, tail, and harness. Ranger was caught, and had a fine collar of blue and red, with a large bow put on, and Herbert's little dog Ponto was made splendid, by tying bright strips to his long white hair all over him.

The carting was going on, and rakers were soon called for. The field was cleared; the wagon was about half full, and it was the last load.

All must mount now, rakes and forks in hand. Not only children,—grandpapa was in, now papa, now mama, now Aunt Lucy, now Aunt Emily, and Uncle John, and Emma, and Harriet. All were in. Charley walked at the head, a long red streamer on his whip. Joe and Roger waited on the stack, streamers on their forks.

"Now hold up your rakes and forks, and shout for the last load," cries Thomas. He was obeyed; there was a famous shout.

They stopped at the stack. "Master must please to get up on the stack, and Joe and Roger must come down."

Grandpapa mounted on the stack; all the rest stood up in the wagon.

"Three cheers for Squire Wakefield! whose hay we have got in this day," cries Thomas.

There were three capital cheers, and then Mr. Wakefield, thanking them, told them supper would be ready in half an hour, and invited them all to partake.

It was a lovely evening, and the long supper table was laid in the garden, on the lawn. The children helped to lay the tables, and were ready and delighted to wait on the company at supper. There was abundance of everything, and the tables looked beautiful when the high vases of flowers and heaped dishes of fruit were placed among the substantial dishes.

The hay was stacked, Smiler put up in the stable, and Thomas and his two assistants, with Charley, had come into the garden; and now the guests began to arrive, —Thomas's wife and three children, Emma's brother and sister, Harriet's father and sister, Charley's old mother, Joe's wife, Roger's mother and sister. There were seats for everybody. Mr. Wakefield and Aunt Lucy took the two ends of the table, and the children waited on all. Everything was so well arranged that they found it quite easy, and when they had no more to do they formed rings on the grass, and danced to their own voices.

Then songs were sung, and the children sometimes joined in chorus, and pleasant stories were told, and they stopped their dance to listen. The sun had gone down in a golden sky, and the moon was up when the happy party separated. The children stayed all night; every sofa and bed was full, and the moon that lighted the other guests to their several homes, peeped in at the windows of Mr. Wakefield's cottage on many little eye-lids fast closed in sleep after a very merry day.

ROSE AND HARRY.

On the sloping side of a green hill there was a pretty cottage, with a little garden round it, and a white gate that led into a wood of firs and larches, mixed with a few birch trees, that sent out a delicious odour after a shower of rain when the sun came out, and the green leaves glistened in the light. It was such a solitary place that this cottage would have been lonely, but that near it there was a farm-house, and the sheep belonging to the farmer used to crop the grass on the hill, and often come close up to the gate; and he had cows in the meadows below, and corn-fields at a little distance, and fine strong horses for his ploughs and wagons, and a pigeon-house on the roof of his barn.

In the cottage there lived a little girl and boy called Rose and Harry, with their mama. Their papa died

ROSE AND HARRY.

when they were too young to remember him, and their mama seemed to have no happiness but in teaching them, walking about the beautiful country with them, giving them pleasure, and trying to make them as good as she told them their dear papa was. They were very happy children, for they were always with their mama, whom they loved so much. When they awoke in the morning they were sure to see her near their little beds. She bathed and dressed them with her own hands. Her voice led their morning prayer. She sat on the hill while they ran and jumped in the fresh sweet air. They sat at the same round table at breakfast with her, and then went with her to see what Mary the maid was doing, to help to give out what was wanted from the store-room, and to see what vegetables were ready to cut in the garden. Then they did their lessons, read to her, wrote, and did sums; and when work was over they played till she called them to dinner, when they had a great many things to talk over with her. Then, after dinner she took them long walks into beautiful places, through woods and green fields, and up hills, where they saw lovely views, and down into deep valleys by the side of clear streams; and when evening came they went home to tea. In sum-

I

mer evenings, when they came in sight of their peaceful
home it was still quite light, and the sun was making
the windows glitter through the roses that grew round
them; but in spring and autumn it was often nearly dark;
the stars were coming out, and the bright light of the nice
warm fire in their sitting-room shone out pleasantly in
the cold air. In winter their walk ended earlier, and
they had to run to keep out the frost, or to skip along
over the snow. But whether it was warm or cold, light
or dark, it was always happy to them. They thought
that they liked better than anything in all their pleasant
lives the time when they sat down to tea, sometimes by
the open window, sometimes by the cheerful fire; and
then, when the table was cleared, and their mama
brought out her work, and told them stories, or taught
Rose to hem and Harry to draw, how happy they were!
The only thing that seemed sad to them was when bed-
time came; but still, the moment their mama said, " It is
time to go to bed," they put everything away, and followed her up stairs; for whatever she wished them to do
they did instantly. They loved her so much, that to
please and obey her was their delight.

It was early in the month of February, when, one day,

they were agreeably surprised by receiving a present from the farmer's wife of a cock and five hens. There was a yard, with an empty hen-house at the back of their cottage, and their mama had often said she should like to keep some fowls to lay fresh eggs for them; so this was a very kind present. Every morning and afternoon they used to go and feed their new pets, and to look for eggs in the nests of the hen-house; and they almost always found three or four a day. They named the cock Emperor, because he looked so grand and proud; the two white hens they named Fairy and Lily, the black one Jet, and the two speckled ones Browny and Pet.

It happened that one day, when Rose and Harry were at play in the garden, they could see their mama's face as she sat at work near the window, and it seemed to Rose that her dear mama looked very pale and melancholy. Rose left off laughing and talking, and was silent so long, that Harry asked what she was thinking of.

" I wish," said she, " that we could do anything useful."

Harry looked as if he did not quite understand her.

" Mama is always working for us, and doing things to

i 2

make us happy," she continued, "and I wish we could do anything to help her."

"So do I, Rose. What can we do?"

This led to a great deal of talk between them; and at last they ran to their mama to ask her to let them try to be useful to her. She smiled, kissed them, and said, "It helped her best to see them try to be good;" but she added, "As you grow older you shall both learn more and more to be useful."

"Let us begin now, mama," said Rose.

"I think that I can find something for you to do for me," answered her mama, "that will be very useful, if I can trust you. It will require care and attention."

Both declared they would be careful and attentive.

"I know by several signs," continued their mama, "that the little white hen you call Fairy wants to sit."

"Does she, and will she have some chickens?"

"I hope so; but sitting hens require great attention when there is no separate place for them to make their nest in. The other hens try to drive them off, to lay their eggs in the nest; then they fight, and perhaps break the eggs. I shall therefore have a door made to shut in Fairy when she has got her eggs under her."

"But how is she to get her food?"

"That is what I am going to trust you with. She must be allowed once a day to come off her eggs, to take her food and have a little exercise. Some one must open her door every morning. She will know how long she may safely stay out. When she goes back she must be shut in again."

"Then may we open her door, feed her, and wait till she is ready to go back?" said Rose.

"And shut her in again when she goes back? How I shall like doing it," said Harry.

"It will be very useful to me if you will take this charge," said their mama. "Mary has not time for it, and it would be troublesome to me."

"We will be very attentive. It will be so very nice!" said Rose.

"But remember," added her mama, "that Fairy must sit three whole weeks; and that, if you forget to let her out even one day, she will suffer much and be very hungry and thirsty; while, if you neglect to let her in again, the eggs will get cold and we shall have no chickens. May I trust you?"

Both declared that she might; that they would never

forget. Accordingly the carpenter put a little wooden door before one of the nests, with holes in it for air. Then Rose and Harry went with their mama to the store-room, and she took thirteen eggs in a little basket. Fairy was already in the nest, though she had no eggs; but Harry took her off and held her while his mama put clean straw and a little hay nicely in. Rose laid all the eggs carefully among it, and then Fairy was allowed to go in. She began to arrange the eggs with her feet and beak, till they were laid as she liked, then she spread her wings out and settled down upon them. The door was now closed and she was left alone.

Next morning before breakfast, Rose and Harry went to the hen-house with a saucer of water, and some barley which they spread on the floor. When they opened Fairy's door and called her she got off, picked it up, and drank some water. They felt the warm eggs, and then shut the door, lest another hen should get in; but they waited in the yard while Fairy wandered about, till, in less than ten minutes, she came to her nest again, when they opened her door, let her in, and then shut her up safely. They went on every morning in the same way. Sometimes it seemed to them that she staid out very long, but they always found she came back before the eggs had lost their warmth; however, to pass the time, they went into the garden and played there, going back every few minutes to see if Fairy was clucking outside her door and ready to go in.

Eighteen days passed on. By this time their mama had told them there was in each egg, she hoped, a chicken, ready in a few days to burst the shell and come out. In three days more they might expect the chickens; indeed Mary told them that in her last place she remembered a hen brought out her brood a day too soon; and therefore, though their mama said she thought there must be some mistake about this, they even hoped for them in two days.

On the nineteenth morning they let out Fairy as usual, shut her door, and went into the garden to go on with their play. The game was keeping a shop on a bench under a large walnut tree. It was such a shop as there was in the village, where they sometimes went with their mama, in which many different kinds of things were sold. For several mornings they had been collecting their stock: now they were ready to begin buying and selling; so that it would be still more amusing to play. They had

scraped sand off the walk, and this they called moist
sugar; some chalk they had found in a field, cut into
pieces was loaf sugar; the black seeds in the laburnum
pods, which were falling as the young spring leaves came
out, were coffee; the dry beech leaves broken up in their
hands made tea; large stones were loaves, and little pebbles rolls; willow twigs peeled and cut into pieces were
pounds of butter; straws cut short, and tied six or eight
together, were candles; and pieces of broken cups and
saucers that Mary gave them, were ranged along, and
made a fine show of crockery ware. Harry was to be
shopman, and Rose customer.

"Stop a moment," said Rose, as Harry placed himself behind the counter; "let me run and look after
Fairy."

She ran back, but soon returned saying Fairy was still
out, and the eggs as warm as pies, and they began to
play. Rose bought several things. She pretended that
she was a farmer's wife who had a large family of children, and wanted to lay in stores for three months, and to
buy a great many cups and plates. Harry praised his
things very much, and she said they were dear and not
good, in the way they had observed people did when they

went to the shop. They played in this way for some time.

"I now want some moist sugar, sir," said Rose.

Harry began to weigh some sand in a pair of scales that their mama had made of orange peel. Rose asked the price, and was beginning to complain of it.

"Your sugar is—Fairy! Oh Harry, Fairy!" she cried, instead of what she was going to say.

The scales dropped from Harry's hands. A long while had passed. They both ran to the hen-house.

Poor Fairy was wandering restlessly before the closed door, ruffling her feathers, and sometimes flying up and pecking at it. Rose opened it. The eggs felt quite cold to her hand. Fairy jumped in and settled on them instantly.

"Run to mama, Harry," cried Rose, the tears filling her eyes. "Ask her to come. See if she can do anything."

Harry ran into the cottage, and brought back his mama, followed by Mary.

"Oh Miss Rose!" said Mary, "what a pity. The eggs must all be spoiled."

"Do you think so?" sobbed Rose. "Oh mama, mama, how sorry I am!"

K

"Might they be put near the kitchen fire?" asked Harry, with a faltering voice.

Their mama put her hand under Fairy, and felt the eggs.

"They are not quite cold," said she; "I yet hope they may not be spoiled."

"Do you think so, mama? Oh how happy I should be," said Rose, looking up in her tears.

"And then perhaps the poor little chickens are not all dead," said Harry.

"We must leave Fairy quiet. That is all we can do," said their mama. "Let us go in to breakfast."

The children each took one of her hands, and walked silently by her side. As they looked up at her they saw that she looked very sad. They sat down, but could not eat: their hearts seemed too full. Rose soon left her seat, threw her arms round her mama's neck, and leaned her head on her shoulder, and Harry went to her also, and laid his head on her lap.

"You will not be able to trust us any more," said Rose.

"And we have not been useful to you at all," added Harry.

"My dear children," she replied, "this is a great disappointment to me. It grieves me that you have failed in the duty you had undertaken. But learn from your failure a lesson that I hope you will never forgot. Whatever duty you have to perform let that be your first concern. Never let pleasure make you forget it."

"We will try, mama," said Rose; and Harry added, "I hope we shall be able to remember."

They went to their lessons. They had never felt so melancholy before, and they were not able to play at all. Their mama took them a long walk, and talked with them, and told them some stories that encouraged them to be earnest in faithfully doing whatever they knew they ought to do.

Next morning, when they were dressed, they stood doubtfully looking at their mama. They were not sure whether she meant to trust them any more; and when she told them to go and let Fairy out they felt grateful to her. They could not help hoping that even this morning some of the chickens might have come out, as Mary had said they might. They looked anxiously in, but the eggs lay as they had always done; no chickens had come out yet. They did not think of play, but remained near the door till Fairy came back to it.

Many were the questions they put to Mary that day as to her expectations, and many a guess did they make between themselves as to the next day. When morning came, the twenty-first morning so long expected, they felt afraid to go to look at the eggs, so fearful were they that no signs of chickens would be there. How differently they would have felt if they had not forgotten their work that unlucky morning. They begged their mama to go with them, and she agreed.

They opened the door; Fairy seemed unwilling to move, and their mama was obliged to lift her off. They watched with beating hearts, but were disappointed. No egg was even chipped, and no chickens were to be seen.

"Do not quite despair yet," said their mama. "Any time to-day or in the night they may come. It was not unlikely, after such a check as the eggs had, that there might be some delay. You must shew your self-denial by not coming to disturb Fairy. The best thing we can do for her is to let her quite alone." When they had shut her in again they went to breakfast, with many fears, notwithstanding their mama's words of comfort. They obeyed her by not returning to the nest, and only went the last thing before going to bed, with her permission, to listen for a chirp. But all was quiet.

Again, when morning came they begged of their mama to go with them, to help them to bear it, if there was no hope. All three went, and Rose with trembling fingers opened the door. "O look! look!" cried Harry in a tone of joy. He had seen a little bright black eye peeping from under Fairy's wing. And now they saw another, and two or three beaks. All was safe. The eggs had not been spoiled.

Before anything more could be done, they both threw their arms round their mama, kissed her, and almost danced for joy. She then lifted Fairy up, pecking and screaming, and put her on the floor to eat her barley. In the nest there were nine pretty little soft chickens, looking like balls of down, some entirely yellow, others speckled with brown, one quite black. There was, besides, an egg with a beak poking out at one end, and another cracked at the end.

Rose and Harry wanted to run for some food; but their mama said it would be better to wait till the rest had come out, for that young chickens did not require to be fed for several hours after they were hatched. She removed

the broken shells, and shook the eggs gently that shewed
no signs of cracking, and by doing so found they were
bad and threw them away. How happily Rose and
Harry went to breakfast now! Still more happy were
they when their mama told them that she meant to trust
them with the care of the young brood. They felt that
they should never forget the lesson they had received,
and were not afraid to take the charge. She gave them
the proper food, and shewed them how to set about their
work. When they returned to Fairy in the afternoon,
they found the two remaining chickens had come out,
and they took her down and put all on the ground, and
had the great pleasure of seeing the little things begin
to peck and to drink water. By their constant care they
reared all the chickens but one, which hurt itself in trying to get through a narrow slit in the gate and died;
but all the other ten grew up. Every morning and afternoon, Rose and Harry took them their food, and Mary
often said, as she looked at them, that she never saw
chickens thrive so well. They got so strong that they
used to stray away, and it often took Fairy some time
before she could collect more than two or three round
her; but all were sure to come at last. Everything went

on as happily as before with Rose and Harry; they enjoyed their game in the garden and all their other plays, but they often remembered their mama's words, and tried never to let pleasure make them forget their duty.

THE FIRST DAY AT THE SEA.

———◆———

"RAMSGATE! Ramsgate!" was called by the man at the station, as the train stopped.

"Ramsgate!" repeated a little boy in one of the carriages, waking up out of a sound sleep.

"Why, Johnny, you have been asleep," said his elder sister Helen; "and Louisa asleep too! Wake up. We are at Ramsgate."

"Where's the sea?" said Johnny, rubbing his eyes.

"It is quite dark," answered his papa, who was already out of the carriage. "Nothing can be seen till to-morrow. Make haste, little Johnny: I will carry you."

In a minute Johnny was seated in a fly, his sisters beside him, then their mama, and their papa on the box. Joseph the groom was seeing the luggage put on a truck; the bell rang, the engine began to puff and blow like

A VISIT TO THE SEA-SIDE.

some great animal preparing to start off again with his load, and away went the train.

"Where are Neptune and Spot?" asked Louisa, putting her head out at the window.

"I hear them barking. Joseph has got them safe out of the train," answered her papa, as they began to move on.

This family came from Warwickshire, which is a long way from the coast, and the children had never yet even had a sight of the sea. They looked out on both sides as they drove along, but in vain; the night was very dark, and they could see nothing. They heard, however, a grand sound, such as they had never heard before, which their mama told them was the sound of the waves; and the air felt very fresh. They presently stopped at a door, which was quickly opened and they got out. It was very nice to go up an unknown staircase, to peep into a strange drawing-room, then to go up to the bed-rooms, where everything was new to them. They thought the beds and curtains very white and clean, and were very glad to see their nurse again, who had gone on a day before them, and had everything ready; and as it was too dark to see out of the windows, they began to long for nothing so

L

much as to lie down in the comfortable white beds; so, before half an hour was over, all three were fast asleep.

Hour after hour passed, while kind sleep was changing them from wearied travellers into active, merry children once more; but they knew nothing of this time. It seemed to them like the next minute that they heard a voice say— "Who wants to look at the sea?" and saw their mama standing in the room, dressed and ready to go out. It was seven o'clock in the morning, and the bright sun was shining on the windows. In a minute Johnny was in her arms, Helen and Louisa by her side, and she took them to the window and drew up the blind.

There lay the beautiful sea before them, under the blue morning sky, sparkling in the sun, the waves gently breaking on the yellow sands. Two fine large ships, with their white sails set, were passing near the shore, and many more in the distance. A steamer was going in the opposite direction. A whole fleet of fishing-boats were coming in towards the harbour, after being out all night. Beyond all, on both sides, and onward as far as the eye could reach, stretched the blue sea, till it met the sky. The children had longed to see it, had wondered what it would be like, had expected it would be beautiful, but it was far greater and more beautiful than they had imagined. They would never forget that first sight of it.

"Make haste and come out to bathe," said their mama.

Very quickly they were dressed, and enjoyed all the delights of choosing a machine, plunging into the refreshing water, dancing and splashing in it, coming out at last to be dried and dressed, meeting their papa on the sands when they came out of the machine, having a good run with him, clambering over some slippery sea-weedy rocks, peeping into a cave in the white cliff, and then going in to breakfast very hungry, and sitting round the table, drawn so near the bow window that they could look out and see what was going on all the time.

The sea was always taking some new and lovely colour; the two ships had sailed out of sight, but three others had come; the tide was rising, and the line of white waves came nearer and nearer; rowing-boats and sailing-boats were scudding this way and that on the sunny water; the steamer for London, which had just started from the pier, passed rapidly across. Then there were donkeys trotting and cantering up and down the sands, with boys and girls on them. In short, it all looked so delightful, that breakfast had hardly been cleared away when their mama told them to get ready and she would take them to spend the whole morning on the sands.

They were not long about getting ready, and went down the cliff by a long wooden staircase. As soon as they got upon the sands they ran to the edge of the sea, stopping only a minute to look at some children who were digging with wooden spades. Neptune and Spot had come out with them, and rushed about barking with joy.

"How nice it is to stand quite near, and have to run back when the next wave comes!" cried Johnny.

"Ah, master Johnny, if you stand so near as that, you will be caught and get wet presently," cried Louisa.

Neptune came bounding past as they spoke, and swam out; they could only see his head bobbing over the waves. He seemed to enjoy it very much; but foolish little Spot would not go out: he only stayed barking by Johnny's side, and when the waves broke on the sands and came hissing up he ran back too. Helen and Louisa were amusing themselves with digging hollows with their hands, and seeing them filled with water, and changed into little ponds, and then covered entirely and lost, one after another, in the great sea.

"Oh Johnny run! run!—what a great wave!" cried Helen.

He ran with all his might, but it was in vain. The wave was too fast for him, and he got wet up to his knees. Neptune swam out at the same time, and shook the water out of his long hair all over him.

"We must go in for dry socks and shoes," said his mama. "But we need not be long about it. As to Neptune's contribution, I can rub that away with my handkerchief."

They went in, but soon got all put to rights and came out again. Passing on towards the stairs they came to a toy-shop, and stopped to look at the things.

"Those wooden spades are exactly like what the boys were digging with," said Johnny. "*Will* you buy us one, mama?"

She answered by going into the shop and telling him to choose one, and greatly added to his pleasure by telling Louisa to choose one also.

"May Helen have one too?" said Louisa.

"I am afraid she is too old for a wooden spade," replied her mama, smiling.

But Helen declared she was not at all too old, and the

shopman said he often sold spades to young ladies of her age; so she also had one, and all three sallied forth, and went down the cliff in great glee. They began to dig as soon as they reached the hard sands. At first they only dug holes; but after a while Helen proposed that they should make a house standing in a garden, with a wall round it. She was to build the house, while Louisa and Johnny made the wall of round white stones, of which they found plenty. They drew a line to shew the boundary, and fixed a row of stones in it. The sand Helen dug out to build the house left a hollow, which they decided should be a pond in the garden, and they planned several walks and a grass-plot, on which they determined to lay green sea-weed, such as they had seen on the rocks.

"How pretty a grotto would look in one corner!" said Louisa.

Both the others thought so too; they therefore left their work, and began to look for shells.

"I have found a lovely little yellow one," cried Helen.

"So have I, and a black one," said Johnny.

Louisa also found a few; but, after searching some time, they had only collected a small number, and these nearly all yellow; so they gathered round their mama, who was all this time sitting reading on a block of wood, with Neptune and Spot by her side, and asked her what they should do for shells. The house, they declared, would be nothing without the pretty grotto, and they could scarcely find any.

Just at that moment there came towards them a boy who carried a flat board slung round his neck covered with beautiful large shells; he came up to their mama, asking her to buy some.

"O how lovely!" cried Helen.

"But they are too large for the grotto," said Johnny.

The boy said he had plenty of smaller ones, which he sold by the pint; and, setting down his board, he took a canvas bag out of his pocket, which was full of all sorts of common shells, white, yellow, pink, and black. These were exactly what the children wanted, and their mama bought a pint for them.

"But where do you find all these?" asked Helen. "We could see none almost, but a few little yellow ones."

The boy said he came from Pegwell Bay, where there were numbers of them; but, he added, he did not find the large ones there. They came from foreign parts, and were brought home by his father, who was a sailor. "Would not the lady please to take one?" he said. He had slung on his board again, and held one in his hand towards her as he spoke. She bought two, and gave him the price he asked; and, after thanking her, he went on.

The grotto was now commenced in good earnest. A layer of stones was first put down, and then the shells raised on it, the largest at the bottom. It took a good while to sort them into different sizes and colours, and then to produce the proper effect by arranging them well. At last, nearly the whole collection had been used up, and the grotto was rising to a peak at the top, when they were startled by a most unexpected event. A wave, pushing on before its companions, sent a pointed flood of water into the midst of their garden, and, rolling back, left their pond full. They had not observed, in their eagerness over their work, that the tide had risen fast, and that their house and garden now stood at the very edge of the sea. They started up; but, while they stood staring in consternation, on came another wave, swept away the grotto, and carried the shells back with it. Scarcely, however, was there time to feel the misfortune, when another, rolling on, brought them back and laid them at their feet.

"Save the shells,—pick them up,—mama, come and help us!" was shouted by all three, while each gathered up as many as the returning waves would leave time for. Their mama had been so much engaged with her book, that she had not observed what was going on; but she came quickly and helped as well as she could. She was obliged, however, to prevent Louisa and Johnny from attempting to save as many as they wished, lest they should be carried away themselves. By great exertions, and at the cost of getting their shoes full of water, they collected a good many; the two dogs came and barked and rushed about as if they wished to help, but did little else except splashing everybody with salt water. When the hurry was over, Johnny began to look very sad, and Louisa could hardly help crying. Fortunately the spades were safe; Helen had thrown them as far away as she could at the first appearance of danger, and they lay on the dry sand; as to the house and garden, it had vanished for ever.

They turned homewards, for it was time for dinner; when they got in, nurse said, she did not know what was

M

to be done for shoes and stockings if they went on in this way; but they told her they should be wiser soon, when they began to understand the ways of the sea. At dinner they related all the adventure to their papa, who advised them to measure their shells and see how many they had saved. They got a pint jug for the purpose, and found that they had not saved above half their stock.

"Suppose," said he, "that we were all to go to Pegwell Bay in a sailing boat this afternoon, and you were to pick up shells for yourselves?"

Great joy was shewn at this proposal. To go out in a boat was pleasure enough of itself, and to gather shells was equally delightful; so they were soon ready, and went to the pier, where they found plenty of boats.

The boats were very pretty, painted of different colours, with gay little flags, and all had names; and as the children looked down at them they began to choose which they should like best. The "Sea-flower" was a pretty name; but then, the "Water-witch" was such bright green and white; the "Sally" did not please them at all,—they would have liked to go in the "Victoria;" but the "Princess Royal" was so pretty altogether, both name, colour, and flag,—for it was painted light cane-colour, with a little black about it, and had a sky-blue flag, and the whitest possible sails,—that they fixed upon it.

They had a delightful sail. There was sufficient breeze to make their boat go dancing over the water, and yet it was warm and pleasant. It was great fun to land at Pegwell Bay, and to scatter over the beach picking up shells; and they found numbers,—in some places the whole beach seemed composed of them. When at last their papa called them to go back to the boat, they found they had filled all the little baskets they brought. As they walked along they passed a row of cottages, and, at the door of one of them, saw the boy standing of whom they had bought the shells in the morning. There was a nice fire in the room of the cottage, and his mother was getting tea ready. They stopped and spoke to him, and shewed him their shells, and their papa thought some of the large ones he saw on the board, that now stood on a table, so beautiful that he bought six of them, which seemed to please the boy very much.

The sun was setting behind Ramsgate when they reached the pier, and a golden light was spread over everything, while the sea looked dark-violet colour; and it was difficult to say whether it looked most beautiful now, or

M 2

when they saw it first, under the blue morning sky, or afterwards in the many changes that came over it during their happy visit to Ramsgate.

A HAPPY SUNDAY.

OLD MARY JONES.

In that part of North Wales which borders on England there are many beautiful grassy hills, often wooded half way up their sides, and lovely green valleys between them. The hills are not too high or rugged to be easily climbed in a morning's walk, and it is delightful to rest on their tops. The air is very fresh; there is a scent of wild thyme growing among the grass on which you tread, and a wide view over all the neighbouring country.

A large and pleasant old house, partly overgrown with ivy, near the top of one of these hills, was the home of Walter and Lucy Lewis. There were pleasure-grounds and plantations all round the house, and the hill had many walks and terraces cut in it, where there were beautiful places, sometimes among trees, sometimes among heath, and ferns, and gay fox-gloves, and

always some new view of the green valley beneath. Mr.
Lewis was the landlord of most of the farms that lay
near, and of most of the white cottages that peeped
out every here and there from some thicket or knoll.
He was a kind landlord to all his tenants, and was especially careful of his cottagers. He never let a cottage
that was badly built, or inconvenient, or made with only
one room in it for a whole family, as some cottages are;
he always had three rooms at least in his, besides a
wash-house, a place for coals and wood, and a pig-sty;
and with each he always gave enough ground to grow
the vegetables for the family. It was a pleasure to see
how clean and comfortable these cottages were. There
was sure to be a side of bacon hanging from the beams
in the kitchen; a good sack of potatoes in a corner; a
large home-made loaf or two of good brown bread, and
comfortable furniture. Whenever sickness or trouble
came upon any of Mr. Lewis's tenants they were sure to
find friends in him and Mrs. Lewis, and whenever any
good fortune or happiness came to them they were glad
to see these good friends come to their gates that they
might relate it. Mr. Lewis had built schools for their
children, and took great pains about their education, and

he had given a large piece of ground to be free for games, for keeping May-day, and other pleasures.

Walter and Lucy were allowed to roam about a good deal by themselves, because every one in the neighbour-hood knew them, and would take care of them. Their mama used to tell them, whenever they went far from home they should look out for the church steeple, for the church stood on the same hill with their house. With this landmark to prevent their losing themselves, they used to take long walks together sometimes. One day they had gone to the top of a low hill that rose next to that on which their house was, and they came to a hedge. There was a gap in the hedge, near the ground, and through this Walter said he would go.

"Now look, Lucy," said he, "how cleverly I shall creep through feet foremost. My feet are through,—now my knees, now——" he disappeared, and not a word more came.

"Walter! Walter! where are you?" cried little Lucy, peeping through. "Oh, Walter, where are you gone?" She went on with a faltering voice, for she saw that the hedge was at the top of a steep bank, and that he must have slipped down at once to the bottom.

"Lucy," said a voice a long way below, "come down here!"

"I cannot," answered she at first; but after a little encouragement from Walter, who now appeared from among some bushes into which he had rolled, she cautiously made her way through the gap, and partly sliding, partly running, soon joined him where he stood. Below them was a small lake which they had often seen in their walks, but never had gone close to, and which looked very inviting, and Walter determined to go down to it. Lucy was afraid. She said they had already lost sight of the steeple, and how should they find their way back? But Walter declared that nothing could be easier than to climb up the bank the way they came down; so, leading his little sister by the hand, and helping her over difficult places, he soon reached the lake with her.

Here everything was very beautiful. There were a great many bright flowers, of which they gathered several, and a number of dragon-flies that flitted over the water with their lacy wings, and their corselets glancing green, gold, and purple in the sun. Walter and Lucy ran along the edge of the lake, watching the quick movements of the dragon-flies, till, suddenly stopping, Lucy declared it was growing dark and she wanted to go home.

"Dark!—Why, how can you say so?" said Walter. "It was only three o'clock when we came out." But, as he spoke, he looked up, and saw that the sky had become covered with black clouds.

They began directly to clamber up the hill, and reached the top at last; but when they looked round, everything was strange. No steeple was in sight, nor did they see any tree or rock that they knew.

"We must have come up the wrong way," said Walter. "But don't be frightened, Lucy dear; let us get down to the lake again and look well about us, so as to find the way we came."

Trying to keep her courage up, Lucy took hold of his hand, and they were soon by the water again. It was easy to them, used as they were to clambering, to go safely down steep places. When they reached the borders of the lake, they saw some large drops of rain falling into the water, and immediately afterwards they were startled by a loud clap of thunder.

"Make haste; let us find the way if we can," said Walter.

N

"I am so tired I cannot go on," said poor little Lucy, beginning to cry.

The rain now poured down, and a flash of lightning darted across the hill, followed by a clap of thunder still louder than the first.

"Oh mama, mama!" sobbed Lucy. "What shall I do? I wish we were at home with you."

"What now?—Dear heart!—what's amiss?" cried a voice behind her.

Both the children turned round, but saw no one. They were standing a little way from the edge of the lake, and a thicket of bushes was between them and it. The voice seemed to come from among them. Lucy clung to Walter in her fear. There was another clap of thunder.

"Come to the door; come in, then," cried the voice. "Heart alive! why do you stay out in the storm?"

"There must be a cottage near us," said Walter; "come with me."

Lucy tried to hold him back, for she was afraid of this strange voice; but he gently pulled her forward, and on the other side of the bushes, close to the edge of the lake, they came to the door of a very small, miserable looking cottage. He opened the door by the latch and they went in. It was so dark in there, that at first they saw nothing; but presently they could distinguish in one corner an old woman lying in a little narrow bed.

"Dear heart!" she exclaimed, as they stood together by her bed; "why, it's the little lady and gentleman from the house."

"Are you not old Mary Jones?" asked Walter.

"Yes indeed, sure I am," she replied. "Sit down, poor little dears. I would help you to take off your wet clothes, but I cannot move this many a day with the rheumatics."

She talked very kindly to them, and told them which corner to sit down in, where the rain would not come through. She had nothing to give them, she said, till her daughter and her grandson came in from work.

The two children sat down, and forgot their own little troubles entirely, so much greater did poor Mary Jones's appear. How miserable, it seemed to them, she must be lying there alone all day long, not able to move, with no one to help her, in this dark, damp cottage. Walter said something to her which shewed he was thinking so.

N 2

"It is a poor place," she replied. "We have no kind landlord to take care of our cottages, as your good papa does. Ours seldom comes into the country."

"But how long have you been so ill?" said Walter. "I remember seeing you in church in your red cloak a few months ago."

"Yes, sure you did," said she. "But I am afraid I shall never go to church again. I have been ill and not able to get up this three months."

"Poor Mary Jones!" sighed little Lucy.

All this time the rain poured down, and the thunder rolled; but it became more distant, and gradually the storm ceased. At the first gleam of sunshine the children began to think of going home, for they knew their mama must be uneasy about them; but they felt as if it was cruel to leave the old woman all alone, though they could do her no good. Meanwhile she tried to make them understand which way they ought to go; but it seemed difficult to make it out.

While they stood waiting and hesitating what to do, footsteps were heard outside, and Mary Jones's daughter and grandson came in, wet through, for they had walked home through the pelting rain.

"Ah! here's little Davy now, can take you the right way," said Mary.

They could not bear to take him out, but he made nothing of it; he said he should soon be home again; so they set off with true feelings of gratitude to these kind people, and glad to see that Mary Jones would soon have some tea and be attended to; for her daughter began to prepare things directly.

They were surprised to find how short a distance it was to get home, now they knew the way. They were soon there; but they found that their mama had been very uneasy about them, and she told them they must not wander so far away any more. They had begged of Davy to wait for a little while; and when they told their mama all about poor Mary Jones, and how kindly Davy had led them home in his wet clothes, she ordered him a good hot supper, and gave him a nice thick warm jacket to put on instead of his wet one; and she put up in a basket a piece of meat and bread, and some tea and sugar, to take to his grandmother.

Still, though all this was a great pleasure to Walter and Lucy, they thought very much about poor old Mary. When little Lucy lay down in her warm bed she sighed, and looked very sad, and when her mama came to give her a kiss, the last thing before she went to sleep, she said, "I wish poor Mary Jones's cottage was warm and dry." Walter dreamed that the lake overflowed, and the water came into the cottage; but just as it grew so deep that it would have drowned the old woman in her bed he started up and awoke. Next morning they could not help thinking of her when it was time for her daughter and Davy to go out to work and leave her, and they determined to ask their mama to let them go and see her when they had done their lessons.

When they went with this request to their mama she told them that their papa had already gone to Mary Jones's cottage, and that she would take them to meet him on his return. They soon saw him coming over the hill when they went out, and ran to meet him; and he told them he had proposed to let Mary have one of his cottages that was now empty, rent-free for the first year; and that she had gratefully accepted this offer. Her daughter, Peggy Davids, Davy's mother, was a good worker in the fields, he said, and Davy had got a place at one of the farmers near, that he was to go to next week; so he expected they would be able to live very comfortably, if they were placed in a cottage that was fit for people to live in, instead of their wretched damp one with only one dark room, and not a morsel of garden.

The children were quite delighted to hear all this; and Mrs. Lewis said she knew old Mary Jones used to make something herself, by knitting the soft Welsh wool into socks and stockings; she remembered buying some of her. Mr. Lewis said she had told him so, and that, if she could get the use of her hands again, she could get her work back.

They went to see the cottage. It was a nice little place, standing high and dry on a hill side, with its garden in front, and white and clean inside and out. Mary Jones, Peggy Davids, and Davy were established in it before a week was over. Mrs. Lewis gave them several little things to help them to furnish it; and, as Davy's wages soon began to come in, and his mother had constant work, they bought more things, and it looked as bright and comfortable as the old place had looked dismal.

But the greatest change was in Mary Jones herself. She had not been three days in her new abode when she declared the pain had gone out of her joints, and that she was able to sleep instead of lying awake all night. In a week she could turn on her side and use her hands; and a few days afterwards Walter and Lucy went to see her, and found her sitting by the fire knitting.

It was about a month after this time, on a fine Sunday morning in autumn, that Mr. and Mrs. Lewis, with a young lady who was on a visit to them, and Walter and Lucy, were going to church, and noticed among the people going along the path before them an old woman in a bright red cloak and black bonnet, leaning on a younger woman with a nice warm shawl on, and a little boy cleanly dressed.

"Mama," said Walter, "I do believe that is old Mary Jones, with Davy and his mother."

"And we shall see her in the old place again," said Lucy.

"It really is Mary Jones," answered their mama.

"I am so glad!" said Walter. "This is a happy Sunday morning."

THE VILLAGE FAIR.

THE VILLAGE FAIR.

———◆———

THERE could not be a quieter village anywhere than Southbourn, except once a year, when it was full of gaiety, noise, and bustle. Once a year the Fair was held there, and then nobody would have known that it *was* Southbourn. The cottages that went straggling up the hill were almost hidden from sight by the booths and shows, and nothing of the village could be seen except the church and the clergyman's house.

About half a mile off there lived a little girl named Jessie White, who, together with all the other little girls, and boys too, of the neighbourhood, looked forward to July, the month when the Fair was held, with the greatest pleasure. In that quiet country place there were no fine shops to go to when you wanted to buy anything, and no exhibitions, zoological gardens, and such agreeable

o

places to amuse people; but the Fair came once a year, and for it they saved up their money, and they hoped to enjoy all manner of fine sights when they went to it.

July had come; and the 13th of July had come; and the next day the Fair began. Already there were several preparations. Some booths had been erected in the village, and wonderful things began to come along the road. The house that Jessie lived in was close to the road-side, but none of the windows looked that way. There was, however, one corner of the garden wall from which, if you got upon a wooden bench that was by it, and looked over, you could see all that passed. Here Jessie took her station whenever she had time to leave her lessons and work. She had already heard some heavy rumbling things go by this morning. And now she heard a sound as if something very wonderful indeed was coming. But whatever she expected, what she saw was far more extraordinary. She saw a great wooden caravan painted yellow, with pictures of lions, tigers, bears, and such savage creatures on it, and drawn by a large elephant, on each side of whom walked a man. The elephant came on in a stately manner with his great feet and strong legs, as if he did not care about his load.

She watched him as he passed close by her, and she could see that, though his huge head and long trunk never moved, he looked at her, perched up in her corner, out of his wise little eye. Behind him came another caravan, painted with pictures of wolves, hyenas, jackals, and other animals, drawn by two camels. Their tall necks, with the small head at the end, might have touched her face if they had liked, and they looked so strange that she jumped down, but soon got up again, and saw that two more caravans drawn by horses followed.

"These must be the wild beasts," thought she to herself. She was sure of it, because, besides the pictures, she had heard strange sounds as they passed, of growls, howls, and squeaks. No wild beasts had come the year before. This was a great pleasure indeed!

While she was watching till the caravans were out of sight, a man passed carrying a box, on which was written, "The only real Mermaid!" Jessie was very much puzzled to think how a mermaid could live in a box. She thought they always lived in the sea.

Nothing else came for a long time; so she went to play in the garden, but presently saw a flag moving along behind the trees; so she went to look, and saw that the flag was fastened to the top of a wooden house on wheels, with a door in front. A man smoking a pipe, a woman and child, sat at the door, and two strong horses drew it. On the flag was written, "The greatest Wonder of the Age;" and on the side of the house, "The Irish Giant, and his friend the American Dwarf;" and there was a picture of a giant, about fourteen feet high, and by his side a little gentleman with a sword by his side, who came about to the giant's knee. Jessie supposed they were both inside, and the man in front was the showman; but she thought the giant must be very much crowded.

It was time to go in again, and she saw no more things pass; but she once heard a funny noise, that made her believe Punch was going by, and a great deal of barking, which she was told came from the dancing dogs, who were very tired, and barked for joy that they were near their journey's end.

Next morning she awoke to the happy feeling of a holiday and the Fair, and after breakfast set off with her mama towards the village. The road was thronged with country people in their Sunday clothes; and as they got near they heard the sound of bells, horns, fiddles, drums, and loud voices. The sound of horns became louder than all the rest; and, turning a corner, they saw advancing towards them a line of men on horseback, each blowing a brazen trumpet, and all dressed in grand scarlet coats, with black velvet hats ornamented with ribbons. Presently they stopped their horses and left off playing, and the foremost man began to proclaim with a loud voice, that on the common outside the village there was to be seen the finest collection of animals in the world. The great Elephant from Siam; the Royal Lion and Lioness; the great Bengal Tiger; the Black Bear and the Brown; Wolves and Panthers; a fine set of Monkeys; and a splendid show of Parrots, Mackaws, and Owls. They then began to blow their trumpets again and moved on. Jessie's mama promised her that she should go to see the wild beasts.

When they got to the first booth in the village, they found themselves among a crowd of people buying and bargaining. There was a gingerbread booth, with gilt cakes, parliament, and gingerbread nuts; a confectioner's, with sugar-plums, bull's-eyes, barley-sugar, sugar-candy, and all sorts of sweet things; a jeweller's, with necklaces, bracelets, brooches, and pins; a haberdasher's, with gay ribbons, laces, gloves, and handkerchiefs, and, best of all, a toy-shop.

Here Jessie and her mama stopped to look and admire. Then they went back to the first booths and bought a bagful of gingerbread nuts, sugar-plums, and such things, to give to some of Jessie's little friends. Again they went to the toy-shop. There was a kite that Jessie fancied would please her cousin Arthur very much, and she thought she would buy it; but she doubted between it and a horse on wheels. While she was deliberating, her mama looked at a pretty doll, and gave her the choice of it or a box of bricks, and after thinking a good while, she chose the bricks; so it was wrapped in paper and given into her hand. Still, the question between the kite and horse was not settled, when she heard behind her some shouts of admiration, and found that a conjuror was performing some wonderful tricks; so they went to look at him.

The conjuror had on a peaked hat and loose coat, and had a long beard, and beside him was a clown with a ridiculous red and white dress, who made fun of everything he did, and made him very angry every now and then. The conjuror did the most amazing things. He held up a ball to shew them, and then put it under a cup. He never touched the cup,—that they were sure of,— and yet, when he raised it, the ball was gone, and was under quite another one at the other end of the table. Then he put a sheet of paper into his mouth, all crumpled up, and drew it out, twenty yards long, out of his nose. And, last of all, he swallowed a knife. Always, while he was preparing some new trick, a man kept playing on the Pandean pipes, and beating a drum at the same time.

Behind the conjuror there was a theatre, where there was to be a play at night, and on the other side there was a peep-show. Jessie felt the greatest wish to see into it; so her mama told her she might. Two boys were looking at the last picture in it as she came up, and she heard one of them say, "Oh my! it *is* beautiful!"

She paid her penny, and put her eyes to the glass, and there she saw a grand procession. The show-man told her it was Queen Victoria going to open Parliament. "There she sat," he said, "in her carriage, with her Crown upon her head, and her Sceptre in her hand, and the eight cream-coloured horses to draw her; and after her came the Royal Children in a carriage with four black horses; and then all the lords and ladies of her court, and the Royal Life Guards to guard her." All this disappeared; and there were the gold workings in California, with a man carrying a lump of gold half a hundred weight on his back, and all the hills and rivers shining with gold. Then came St. Paul's and the Tower of London. Afterwards, the Lord Mayor and Lady Mayoress, the Aldermen, Sheriffs, and their ladies, taking water at London Bridge, to go up the river in the State Barge. Then a view of Edinburgh, with the castle-rock rising in the middle, and the sea in the distance. And there were a great many views in the peep-show besides. Jessie was very much delighted with it; but her mama told her she must not quite believe all the showman told her about California, nor exactly about all the other things; she must only remember it as something very amusing.

Jessie now went back to the toy-shop and bought the kite. It was time to go home, and much more remained to be seen; but her mama made her happy by telling her that she should have another holiday to-morrow, and that her cousin Arthur had promised to come, so that they could enjoy all the other sights together. Foremost among these were the wild beasts. Some friends they met in the Fair told them the animals were very fine indeed. Jessie asked them if they had seen the mermaid, but they had not heard of it.

" Oh!" said a boy standing near, "it's not a live mermaid,—only a dead one; and I believe that it's nothing in the world but a stuffed monkey with a fish's tail glued on it, and a green wig."

Jessie no longer wished to see it; but she was delighted at the prospect of having Arthur with her, and of going to the wild beasts. She found Arthur already arrived when she went home. He was very much pleased with his kite, and they were very happy together next day, and enjoyed the sight of the elephant, lions, tigers, and all the other creatures. They also had a swing with a great many other boys and girls, and all agreed they never remembered a better Fair than this had been.

P

HOW ROGER CAME BACK AGAIN.

———◆———

ONE summer day a rosy-cheeked country girl was walking along the busy streets of a crowded city. Once or twice she had asked her way, and her last direction made her turn into a narrow lane, and then into a narrower court. A few minutes before, she had been admiring the gay shop windows; now, she had to hold her breath, the air was so dreadfully bad, and to pick her way among black pools and gutters. No fresh breezes, no sunshine, could get in there, and all the poor little children that lived in the dirty houses round looked pale and ill. The young woman asked for No. 10; and when she had found it she inquired for Roger Block, and was shewn into a room where there seemed to be a number of people and children crowded together almost in the dark. Roger was her little brother, and she knew his

ROGER AT THE FARM.

face among them all, long as it was since she had seen him, and sickly as he looked. The poor Irish people he was with had taken him in when his mother died and he was left friendless, and had given him a share of their scanty stock of food and their little room, though there were a man and his wife, six children, and an old grand-father, with only that one dark room to live in. He was now to go with his sister Nancy to the farm where she was servant: her kind master had asked him. Roger was a grave, quiet boy. He bid his friends good-bye without showing much sorrow; but Nancy's eyes over-flowed as she thanked them for their goodness, and helped the woman to make Roger's face as clean as half a pint of muddy water could make it, and to smooth down his shabby pinafore. He had no packing to do, for the clothes he wore were all he had; so he took his sister by the hand, and they went together to the inn where the wagon that brought her to the town had put up, and started for the farm in it before night.

Roger settled himself on some empty sacks and fell asleep, and there he slept all night, with Nancy and the wagoner's wife, who had come to keep her company, by his side. At five in the morning he was roused, for they were at the farm, and Nancy told him to come with her, for she must go and help the missis to milk the cows.

Roger got out of the wagon. What a new world he was in! Instead of the dark, crowded, stifling room he was accustomed to, he was standing at the gate of a large field. The sun had just risen, and every blade of grass sparkled with dew-drops. The air was full of sweet scents. There was a grove of trees in sight, with cattle lying under them. The village church appeared in the distance. Bright flowers were on the ground. Birds were singing. Never, in all his life, did Roger forget that minute.

He walked by Nancy's side down the field, and she told him that was the missis milking one of the cows; and she showed him how to pull his front hair when he made his bow after he had been spoken to.

"So you have brought your brother," said her mistress, continuing to milk the cow while she spoke. "Be a good boy, and we will see what can be done for you."

At a sign from Nancy, Roger pulled the front lock of his hair and tried to make a bow, and then stood staring out of his large eyes, and thinking he never saw anything so wonderful or pleasant as all this. The sheep-dog came up to him and made acquaintance with him, and then Mrs. Truman told Nancy to carry in the milk pail that was full, and she would soon come with the other. On their way they met Farmer Truman, who was going his rounds of the farm before breakfast, on horseback.

"Well, Nancy," he said, "so that's the boy. Be a good boy, and we shall see what we can do for you."

Roger pulled his hair again. And now he went to the dairy with Nancy. It seemed to him a wonderful place, so clean, airy, and sweet, with numbers of pans of what Nancy told him was milk, standing in rows, and great jars of cream, and multitudes of rolls of butter. But the mistress came in, and then Nancy had plenty to do, and he must wait outside. No matter, however. All was wonder and pleasure to him. There were sheep feeding, and turkeys, geese, ducks, cocks, and hens wandering about. He did not even know the names of these different kinds of poultry. He had never seen any like them, except a few ragged, dirty cocks and hens in the court.

Presently he was called to breakfast in the kitchen, and sat down among the ploughmen and carters. It was

more astonishing than all to see how they ate, and to find
that he could have as much as he wanted, and was eating
too.   There were great slices of bread, bacon, and pud-
ding, and hot coffee with a quantity of milk in it.   After
breakfast he saw the farm-yard, the great hay-stacks and
corn-stacks, and the barns.   Such high places! some full of
corn stored away,—one that looked empty and immense at
first, but in which he soon saw there were all manner of
things, strange to him, and which he admired very
much;—these were various tools and machines, spades,
rakes, hoes, sickles, hay-knives, hay-forks, pitch-forks,
brooms, harrows, chaff-cutters, and numbers of other
fine things.

Then he saw the stables, with the fine, strong, well-fed
horses in their stalls, and saw the men take them out to
their work again; and he saw the large cow-house, ready
for the cows when they were put up in winter, with the
calf-pens in one corner; and he saw the pig-styes, with
all the pigs, large and small.   At dinner and at supper
he had as much as he could eat.   At night he slept at
the wagoner's in a little bed up in the garret; the moon
shone in at the window in the roof when he lay down,
and he saw the blue sky through it when he awoke, and

heard sparrows chirping in the thatch. This was all the greatest wonder and delight to him.

Three days of this kind of life had passed, when Farmer Truman sent for Nancy and Roger.

"I have got an admission for Roger into the Orphan School of our county town," said he. "Your mother longed for you to be a scholar and learn a trade. Be a good boy, and you may make a man of yourself."

Nancy curtsied, and thanked the master. Roger said nothing, and Nancy could not make him understand that he ought to make his bow. That very day his friend the wagoner took him to the school. It was a fine building, with large rooms, and a great many boys. Everything was in good order. Roger was dressed in new clothes, and well taken care of, but he looked very grave, and was thought a stupid boy.

Three evenings afterwards, as the wagoner's wife was shutting her shutter, she heard a tap at the door, and when she opened it there stood Roger.

"Why, Roger, how came you here?" said she.

He only said, "he liked best to be here."

She gave him a scolding for running away, but took him in, gave him some supper, and sent him to bed. The farmer was very angry, would not see him, nor let Nancy speak to him, and sent him back next morning.

Four evenings afterwards there was a tap at the wagoner's door as he and his wife sat at supper; and when they opened it there stood Roger again.

They were very angry this time, and sent him to bed without any supper. The farmer reproved him severely when he sent him back, and told him not to dare to run away again.

A week afterwards, when the wagoner came home from work, he saw Roger sitting under a tree near his door; and this time they would not take him in again at the school.

Nobody knew what to do with him now. His new clothes were sent back to the Orphan School, and his shabby old ones put on. Nancy was in great distress, and Roger was shut up in the garret till the farmer made up his mind about him.

Some kind ladies, relations of the farmer's, who were rich, happened to be at the farm then, and they said they would take the poor boy home. They lived in a town sixty miles off; so it was impossible, they said, he could run back from there. They took him away, therefore, and were very kind to him, clothed him well, taught him to read and write, gave him all his meals beside them, made him walk before them when they walked out, and never let him be out of their sight, except when they went out visiting, and then he was locked into a room with some play-things, and the servants told to take care of him. He seemed contented, and learned fast, but he never forgot his happy days. If he was told about some beautiful place, he asked if it was like the farm. If he read of some great man, he asked if he was as great as Farmer Truman.

Six months of this life had passed, when, one day, Roger was missing and could be found nowhere. The kind ladies wrote to the farm, but many weeks passed and no one saw or heard of him.

At last, one cold, bitter night in winter, a little low tap was heard at the wagoner's door.

"See if that be not Roger!" said his wife.

And Roger it was. Tattered, thin, and wearied, there he stood. He had begged his way and come back all the sixty miles on foot. It was impossible for the good woman to refuse to take him in.

The farmer declared the boy must be an idiot, when

Q

she went to him in the morning with her story; but she said, it was all along of his love of a country life.

"He has no turn, like, for scholarship," said she. "Could not you please to find him some work to do on the farm, and give him a trial?" Nancy looked imploringly through her tears, and Mrs. Truman said a kind word for him; so the farmer consented, and Roger was made cow-boy that very day.

Never was such a change seen as came over him. He brightened up. He showed himself the most active, clever boy that had ever been there. He soon learned to do all manner of things, and was always ready to help at everything. He could harness the horses for ploughing or carting, clean them, feed them, or bring them back. He could feed the pigs and calves, drive the sheep to the fold, and at shearing time, hay-making, and harvesting, was of the greatest use. In short, as the men said, he could lend a hand at anything; and all this was done without neglecting his cows. Before he was sixteen he was made a carter, and drove a team of horses, with a great whip on his shoulder, and a white smock frock on; and no king was ever prouder of his sceptre and his robes. The farmer said he never had a better lad in his service, and he hoped he would never leave it, but grow up to be one of his regular labourers, and have a good cottage, and get a good wife of his own.

LONDON:
W. M'DOWALL, PRINTER, LITTLE QUEEN-STREET,
LINCOLN'S-INN-FIELDS.

CPSIA information can be obtained
at www.ICGtesting.com
Printed in the USA
BVHW070847051020
590305BV00009B/736